Brigade Recruiter's Roster

THE

GEORGE WASHINGTON MEMORIAL BRIGADE

HANDBOOK FOR MINUTEMEN

JAMES HATCHER

ISBN-13: 978-1500395759
ISBN-10: 1500395757

Available from Amazon.com, CreateSpace.com,
and other retail outlets

www.CreateSpace.com/4885613

Printed by CreateSpace, Charleston SC
An Amazon.com Company

THIS ROSTER BELONGS TO

_____

NAME

_____

PHONE

_____

EMAIL

_____

ENCAMPMENT   NO.

_____

LOCATION

DEDICATION

This book is dedicated to all those Freemasons,
who have promised to further the cause of
Freedom and Liberty.

CONTENTS

ACKNOWLEDGMENTS

We wish to acknowledge the supporters and staff of the George Washington Masonic National Memorial in Alexandria, Virginia, and all Freemasons, who have taken up the cause to support the great endeavor of raising funds to repair, restore and maintain this monument of American Heritage.

For less than the price of a cup of coffee or a cheap fast food dollar menu item with tax, a Freemason can join in this effort through this program, and forever be remembered as a right and honourable member of the

GEORGE WASHINGTON MEMORIAL BRIGADE

May you all become General Officers one day. For if you do, we shall have accomplished our mission to the best of our abilities.

1 ABOUT THE BRIGADE

The George Washington Memorial Brigade is a private Masonic group of American patriots, who have chosen to take on the issue of preserving this great monument for all times.

Formed a few days after the 2014 Annual Grand Communication by some Brothers of Rockford Masonic Lodge No. 469 F&AM in Rockford, Tennessee, the concept originated after a failed proposal during the Grand Lodge session to assess each member an annual $1.00 per capita tax to support the monument. The Senior Warden advised that he could not support it. If the Grand Lodges of our Great Nation are going to "tax" their members, like the British taxed the American Colonists, then he felt Bro. George would not have approved of such an endeavor. He stated that, if he wanted to give $20.00 per year to support the Monument, then it would be his personal choice, but he felt it should not be mandatorily imposed upon him to make such a commitment. Several of us agreed, and the Brigade was founded.

With the forming of the Brigade Program, we hope that it will become a regular source of donations through Masonic Lodges to protect our National memorial monument, and at the same time, offering Freemasons a patriotic program to present at Masonic functions.

2 ABOUT THE MEMORIAL MONUMENT

The George Washington Masonic National Memorial is a memorial and museum built and funded by the Freemasons of the United States. Situated in Alexandria, Virginia, the 333-foot neoclassical structure stands foremost as a memorial to the life and character of George Washington. The Memorial is also an active Masonic temple, research library, cultural space, community and performing arts center, and tourist attraction. Facilities are available for visiting Craft lodges and other Masonic bodies to hold meetings, including out- of-state groups. Guided tours are available daily, excluding major holidays. For more information, visit **http://gwmemorial.org.**

History of the Memorial

The two Lodges most closely associated with George Washington are Fredericksburg Lodge at Fredericksburg, Virginia, his Mother Lodge and Alexandria-Washington Lodge at Alexandria, Virginia, where he was elected Charter Master under the Grand Lodge of Virginia. No precise date can be found when the Lodge at Fredericksburg was chartered. The date of its first meeting is usually ascribed as September 1, 1752, under a dispensation from the Provincial Grand Lodge of the Colony of Massachusetts. The Lodge was granted a charter on July 21, 1758, by the Grand Lodge of Scotland. Washington was initiated an Entered Apprentice on November 4, 1752, passed to the degree of Fellow Craft on March 3, 1753, and raised to Master Mason on August 4, 1753.

The Lodge at Alexandria, Virginia was first warranted by the Provincial Grand Lodge of Pennsylvania on February 3, 1783, as Lodge No. 39. George Washington attended a St. John the Baptist Celebration of the Lodge in June of 1784. He was later made an Honorary Member of the Lodge. On April 22, 1788, the Lodge received a Charter from the Grand Lodge of Virginia as Alexandria Lodge No. 22. The Lodge asked Washington to be its Charter Master under the Virginia Charter and he agreed. Washington was inaugurated as the First President of the United States on April 30, 1789 while holding the office of Master of Alexandria Lodge. After his death on December 14, 1799, the Lodge was renamed Alexandria-Washington Lodge No. 22, by the Grand Lodge of Virginia.

Through the generosity of Washington's family and friends, Alexandria-Washington Lodge became the repository of many artifacts of Washington and the Washington family. The Lodge rooms were inadequate for the display and storage of the memorabilia and fire in the Lodge in 1871 destroyed many of the invaluable and significant Washington artifacts.

History is replete with men who, out of necessity, arise to undertake a great enterprise. For this occasion, it was Charles H. Callahan, who in 1909, while Senior Warden of Alexandria-Washington Lodge, purchased several lots on Shuters Hill, which he gave to the Lodge for the site of a fire proof Lodge Hall. Following consultation with and with the urging of the Lodge, Joseph W. Eggleston, the Grand Master of Virginia, invited every Grand Master in the United States to assemble in Alexandria-Washington Lodge on February 22, 1910 for the purpose of forming an association to plan and build a suitable Memorial to George Washington, the Mason.

Representatives from twenty-six Grand Lodges did assemble and approved and endorsed the erection of the Memorial, and The George Washington Masonic National Memorial Association was formed. Thomas Shryock, Grand Master of Maryland, was elected the first President of the Memorial Association.

Ten years after the first official meeting of the Association, the concept of a colossal building as a Memorial "lighthouse" to Washington was approved by the Grand Lodges of the United States. The site was selected because it followed the ancient tradition for the location of temples on hilltops or mountains. It was also located on land with which General Washington was familiar; it was the very spot once proposed by Thomas Jefferson as the ideal site for the nation's Capitol.

The groundbreaking ceremony took place on June 5, 1922. Louis A. Watres, President of the Memorial Association and Past Grand Master of Pennsylvania, and Charles H. Callahan, Past Master of Alexandria-Washington Lodge No. 22, and a future Grand Master of Virginia participated in the ceremony. Despite the great expense, the Memorial Association was determined not to borrow money. Construction only proceeded as money was collected for each stage of the project.

On November 1, 1923, the Memorial's cornerstone was dedicated in a Masonic ceremony. President Calvin Coolidge, former President and Chief Justice William H. Taft and numerous other dignitaries performed the ceremony before a crowd of thousands of Freemasons from around the nation. The onset of the Great Depression did not stop work on the Memorial. For over 10 years, Freemasons steadily and faithfully contributed to the construction of the Memorial. On May 12, 1932, the bicentennial year of George Washington's birth, the dedication of the Memorial took place with President Herbert Hoover participating.

After World War II, work on the Memorial's interior began in earnest. By 1970, the George Washington Masonic National Memorial was completed. In 1999, the large square and compasses were added to the front lawn, a visible sign to the Masonic nature of the Memorial. A repository of many artifacts and the history of American Freemasons, the Memorial remains a lasting monument to George Washington, the Man, the Mason, and Father of our Country.

3 WASHINGTON MEMORIAL SERVICE

Introduction

This ceremony is written for the purpose of honoring Bro. George Washington, and is suitable for performance—with adjustments as needed—in a tiled lodge of any degree.

Washington's Birthday is a Federal holiday in the United States, celebrated on the third Monday of February. His actual date of birth is February 22, 1732. Washington was our first and greatest president and his birthday is properly celebrated on February 22.

Preparation

If the lodge room includes a painting or bust of Washington, it is appropriate for it to be highlighted in some way prior to the opening of the lodge. For example, a wreath could be added to it for the occasion, or a table placed before it to display flowers, a candelabra or an electric lamp. Contact the George Washington Masonic National Memorial gift store to obtain an appropriate image of Washington for lodge display, if needed. Note: Regulations vary.

This ceremony is a template, which should be adapted to the procedures of your jurisdiction prior to any performance. Please contact your appropriate Grand Lodge representative with questions.

A
Ceremony
for the Celebration
of the Anniversary of the
Birth of Brother George Washington

The Worshipful Master may begin by having the lodge called from labor to refreshment according to ritual specified by his jurisdiction.

Wm (rising): Brethren, the time has come for us to honor the memory of Worshipful Brother George Washington, the first President of the United States. As we reverently celebrate the anniversary of his birth, I call upon each brother present to mark well his many virtues as a man and a Mason.

Wm: Bro. Secretary.

Sec.(rising): Worshipful Master.

Wm: You will read the Masonic roll of George Washington:

Sec.:   Born, February 22, 1732.
         Entered, Fredericksburg Lodge, at Fredericksburg, Virginia, November 4, 1752.
         Passed to the Degree of Fellow Craft, March 3, 1753.
         Raised to the Sublime Degree of Master Mason, August 4, 1753.
         Elected to serve as Charter Master of Alexandria Lodge No. 22, December 27, 1788.
         Called to the Celestial Grand Lodge, December 14, 1799, age 67, and for 47 years a brother of the Craft.

(Secretary is seated.)

Wm: Brother Senior Warden.

SW (rising): Worshipful Master.

Wm: You will rehearse Bro. Washington's record of achievement.

SW: Appointed Commander-in-Chief of the Continental Army, 1775.
With final victory of the War of Independence, resigned his commission, 1783.
President of the Constitutional Convention, 1786.
Unanimously elected first President of the United States, 1788.
Unanimously reelected to his second term as President of the United States, 1792.
Retired from the Presidency and returned to Mt. Vernon, 1797.

(Senior Warden is seated.)

Wm: Bro. Junior Warden.

JW (rising): Worshipful Master.

Wm: It is my will and pleasure that you speak to Bro. Washington's undying legacy.

JW: Our illustrious Brother Washington was a man of unparalleled character, as exemplary in private as he was in the public eye. In the language of Freemasonry, he was a just and upright Mason, ever walking and acting according to the noblest principles of our Craft.

It is only natural that many have regarded his life as a "perfect ashlar," a true exemplification of all of the moral attributes of a sincere and authentic Master Mason. As one of our forebears in the Craft so fittingly expressed: Washington "was indeed a paragon in Freemasonry, an exemplar of its virtues and its graces. There is no degree of moral improvement suggested by Masonic teachings to which he did not aspire, and few to which he had not attained."

Bro. Washington was indeed, as we all aspire to be, a "living stone," and to the glory of the Great Architect of the Universe, he remains the cornerstone of the American civilization . . . and not only so for our society, but also for those of other nations who have followed us into the manifold blessings of freedom, liberty and equality.

So is he now and so shall he ever remain American Freemasonry's "grand exemplar," whom countless Freemasons seek to emulate in their own lodges and their own communities. In the mystic tie, his exalted merits live on, met with our inalienable regard! So we honor Bro. Washington, exalt his memory and with heart and tongue celebrate his inestimable legacy to all humanity.

(Junior Warden is seated.)

Wm: General Henry Lee's eulogy to George Washington, the friend of Masonry, of his Country and of Man:

"First in war—first in peace—and first in the hearts of his countrymen, he was second to none in the humble and enduring scenes of private life; pious, just, humane, temperate, and sincere; uniform, dignified, and commanding, his example was as edifying to all around him as were the effects of that example lasting. To his equals he was condescending, to his inferiors kind, and to the dear object of his affections exemplarily tender; correct throughout, vice shuddered in his presence, and virtue always felt his fostering hand; the purity of his private character gave effulgence to his public virtues."

As we culminate our celebration of the birth of our Bro. George Washington, let us ever bear in mind his great works, and above all give thanks to the Supreme Architect of the Universe for his life.

• • • (all rise)

Wm: Bro. Chaplain.

Chaplain: Worshipful Master.

Wm: Let us pray.

Chaplain: Most holy and glorious Lord God, thou Great Architect of heaven and earth, we ask Thy blessing and we give our thanks for your servant George Washington. We are thankful for all that he did as a man, as a Freemason and as the father of our nation. May we always be worthy and grateful for his legacy, and may we remain free to celebrate the birth of such a good man. Amen.

Resp.   So mote it be.

Wm: To Solomon, the luminary of the East, and to Washington, the glory of the West— May the rays of their virtues strike right to the soul of every Freemason."

- (all are seated)

If the brethren are at refreshment, the Worshipful Master now restores the lodge to labor according to normal procedure.

About this ceremony

This ceremonial template is provided by the George Washington Masonic National Memorial for the use and adaptation of lodges around the world that wish to join us in our work to inspire humanity by promoting the virtues, character and vision of George Washington, the man, the Mason and the father of our country.

This ceremony may be updated from time to time. To request the latest version, contact W. Bro. Shawn Eyer, Director of Communications, at shawneyer@gwmemorial.org.

4 ABOUT THE PROGRAM

INTRODUCTION

The George Washington Memorial Brigade is a copyrighted Masonic Lodge Program, designed to be used in-house by Lodges, to raise donations for the George Washington Masonic National Memorial in Alexandria, Virginia.

The Brigade Program is voluntary and is administered by Freemasons. The MasonicPress.com has designed this program for the individual Mason to use, however, it is out hope that it will be selected as one of your Lodge's regular, on-going program activities.

The Brigade has NO National Headquarters, nor personnel, nor dues, nor national structure, nor any other bureaucratic function...and never will. The MasonicPress.com maintains the program copyright, but fully extends usage and adaptation to Freemasons and Masonic Lodges to propel the success of the program in support of this historic national landmark.

THUG WARNING: We will fully prosecute to the extent of the law in United States District Court, any persons or organizations found using the program for non-Masonic purposes and/or to defraud others for their own mercenary motives and scam agendas. This is a Masonic program for Freemasons to administer and operate, benefiting our national monument.

Abuse of the program BY ANYONE will not be tolerated. Unsavories, consider yourselves warned.

HOW THE PROGRAM WORKS

Individual Recruitment

The program may be administered by individual Freemasons. All that is required is you keep a log of who you have "recruited" into the program with their donation amounts.

To recruit a new member:

You may send or give those you know a copy of the Recruiting Letter (optional).

1. Have them select the rank of their choice at their chosen giving level.

2. Accept their donation and place it in a GWMNM Donation Envelope (your Lodge should have some, or they can order some) to be mailed directly to the GWMNM.

3. Administer the Brigade Oath to the new member.

4. Fill out a Writ of Enlistment/Commission Certificate (which can be downloaded for free at masonicpress.com) and give it to the new member with the appropriate New Member Letter (Friend or Brother).

5. Record their information on the Brigade Recruiter's Roster and, if a Masonic Brother, give him a copy of the New Member-Brother letter. Form and letters are downloadable for free at masonicpress.com or you can order a paperback journal from us for a nominal fee to keep your records in.

6. Mail the donation envelope.

Team Recruitment

The program may also be administered by program teams of Freemasons. All that is required is you keep a log of who you have "recruited" into the program. To recruit a new member, follow the same process as Individual Recruitment.

Team recruitment is designed to work best at Lodge or Masonic events, where the team can set up an information table and sign up new members.

Team members can be creative by wearing Continental Army uniforms or colonial clothing, displaying a Betsy Ross Flag, filling out Enlistment Papers with a quill pen, etc. The idea is to be creative, make it fun, and have fun doing it.

If you are a stuffy, serious vending table, do not expect much success. There is enough of that in Masonry now, and it is killing us.

Team Recruiters should have the following for an event:

- American Flag (preferably on a staff in a flag stand)
- Container with GWMNM donation envelopes
- Brigade Encampment Journal (3-ring binder or bound record book – see masonicpress.com)
- Ink pens
- Official Brigade Writ of Enlistment/Commission certificates (printed in color on parchment paper looks best)
- Copies of the Recruitment and New Member-Brother letters.
- Table and at least two (2) chairs.
- Copy of the Minuteman Oath for Enlistment/Commissioning Ceremony
- _____
- _____
- _____
- _____

MEMBERSHIP RANKS

Honorary Ranks

A New Member may enlist in the Brigade to the following Honorary Ranks:

$1	Enlisted as a **MINUTEMAN**
$5 to $9	Enlisted as a **PRIVATE**
$10 to $19	Enlisted as a **CORPORAL**
$20 to $49	Enlisted as a **SERGEANT**
$50 to $99	Enlisted as a **SERGEANT MAJOR**
$100 to $149	Commissioned as a **LIEUTENANT**
$150 to $199	Commissioned as a **SUBALTERN**
$200 to $249	Commissioned as a **CAPTAIN**
$250 to $299	Commissioned as a **MAJOR**
$300 to $349	Commissioned as a **LT. COLONEL**
$350 to $399	Commissioned as a **COLONEL**
$400 to $499	Commissioned as a **BRIGADIER GENERAL**
$500+	Commissioned as a **MAJOR GENERAL**

Promotions

A currently enrolled member may advance in the Ranks by making additional contributions at the appropriate giving level. Donations are cumulative and should be referenced in the Brigade Recruiter's Roster and/or the Brigade Encampment Journal, however, this program operates under the honor system, should evidence of prior donation amounts cannot be located.

Regular Ranks

You can also advance through the Regular Ranks by "recruiting" others into the Brigade.

Individuals aspiring to advances must keep track of their own recruitments and notify other Brigade members in their Team or Lodge when they advance. In a Lodge scenario, it is up to the Lodge to decide if a ceremony should be conducted or not.

There are twelve (12) additional ranks in the Brigade, based on those of General Washington's Continental Army. They are:

Promotion in the Regular Ranks are as follows:

PRIVATE – A Freemason who has personally recruited 25 or more Minutemen into the Brigade;

CORPORAL – A Freemason who has personally recruited 50 or more Minutemen into the Brigade;

SERGEANT – A Freemason who has personally recruited 75 or more Minutemen into the Brigade;

SERGEANT MAJOR – A Freemason who has personally recruited 100 or more Minutemen into the Brigade;

LIEUTENANT – A Freemason who has personally recruited 125 or more Minutemen into the Brigade;

SUBALTERN – A Freemason who has personally recruited 150 or more Minutemen into the Brigade;

CAPTAIN – A Freemason who has personally recruited 200 or more Minutemen into the Brigade;

MAJOR – A Freemason who has personally recruited 250 or more Minutemen into the Brigade;

LIEUTENANT COLONEL – A Freemason who has personally recruited 300 or more Minutemen into the Brigade;

COLONEL – A Freemason who has personally recruited 350 or more Minutemen into the Brigade;

BRIGADIER GENERAL – A Freemason who has personally recruited 400 or more Minutemen into the Brigade;

MAJOR GENERAL – A Freemason who has personally recruited

500 or more Minutemen into the Brigade;

COMMANDER-IN-CHIEF – Sorry, this rank is reserved for General Washington himself.

To progress through the different ranks, all that is required is that you personally recruit new Minutemen into the Brigade. This can be informally or formally, as there are no official "rules" for recruitment.

Presentation of Rank Certificates may be done informally, at your Lodge's Stated Meetings, at District or Grand Lodge functions, depending on the presenting person or body.

FREQUENTLY ASKED QUESTIONS

Q: Who can become a member of the Brigade?
A: Anyone of any age; however, only active Freemasons can become Brigade Recruiters and enroll members.

Q: What is my Encampment and Number?
A: Your Lodge Name and Number or the participating Lodge and Number.
Example:
Rockford Lodge No. 469 F&AM would be Rockford Encampment No. 469

Q: Do I have to purchase the Brigade Recruiter's Roster or Brigade Encampment Journal?
A: No, the printed copies available for purchase from masonicpress.com are for your convenience. You may always use the blank record sheets, downloadable free from masonicpress.com, and keep them in a binder.

Q: Do I have to buy any Brigade materials to administer this program?
A: No. All forms, materials, certificates, etc., are available for free from masonicpress.com for your usage. We do ask that you print ALL certificates on parchment paper, so the new member has a certificate that looks like everyone else's.

Q: When can I work on recruiting new members and collecting donations?
A: You may begin working on the honorary ranks and orders as soon as you become a Minuteman.

Q: Are there any reporting requirements?
A: Not to the Brigade or the Masonic Press. The procedure of mailing donations in the donation envelopes is designed to keep the donation a personal donation to the GWMNM from the contributor, NOT from the Brigade or Lodge. The Brigade Encampment Journal is for recording and tracking the Masonic work of the members participating in the program to record levels of advancement. You should not officially involve the Lodge Treasurer and bank account in the operation of this program. You are not receiving monies into your Lodge. You are collecting donations for the GWMNM and mailing them for someone else.

Q: How does my Lodge participate in the program?
A: Download the required materials for free from masonicpress.com and start spreading the word and recruiting new Minutemen today.

Q: Can my Masonic Lodge use this as a fundraiser and donate a portion of the proceeds to the GWMNM?
A: NO-NO-NO! ALL proceeds are to be mailed to the GWMNM upon receipt from the recruited member.

Q: Who are the Brigade Minutemen?
A: All men, women and children, who have made a donation or had a donation made in their name at any rank level, regular (Freemasons only) or honorary (non-Freemasons of any age).

☐

RECRUITING PROCEDURES

Individual and Team

You should download a blank form or purchase a bound copy of the Brigade Recruiter's Roster (Individual) and/or the Brigade Encampment Journal (Team) to keep track of individual recruitments and donation amounts. Your Lodge Secretary can track and report the amounts collected for your Lodge, as needed or required, when you supply him with a copy of your annual records.

HOW DO I GET STARTED TODAY

It's as simple as 1-2-3...

1. Go to **masonicpress.com > Geo. Washington Memorial Brigade** link.
2. Download and/or order the materials you need.
3. Start recruiting new members.

WHAT IF I HAVE QUESTIONS?

You may contact us online at: **masonicpress.com**

Or, send us an email at: **masonicpressinfo@gmail.com**

or, send us a letter at: **The Masonic Press**
217 Rockford Cedar Street
Rockford, Tennessee 37853-3240 USA

5 RANKS OF THE BRIGADE

Recruit – An American Patriot duly enlisted in the Brigade as a Minuteman;

There are seven (12) additional ranks in the Brigade, based on those of General Washington's Continental Army. They are:

Private – A Freemason who has personally recruited 25 or more Minutemen into the Brigade;

Corporal – A Freemason who has personally recruited 50 or more Minutemen into the Brigade;

Sergeant – A Freemason who has personally recruited 75 or more Minutemen into the Brigade;

Sergeant Major – A Freemason who has personally recruited 100 or more Minutemen into the Brigade;

Lieutenant – A Freemason who has personally recruited 125 or more Minutemen into the Brigade;

Subaltern – A Freemason who has personally recruited 150 or more Minutemen into the Brigade;

Captain – A Freemason who has personally recruited 200 or

more Minutemen into the Brigade;

Major – A Freemason who has personally recruited 250 or more Minutemen into the Brigade;

Lieutenant Colonel – A Freemason who has personally recruited 300 or more Minutemen into the Brigade;

Colonel – A Freemason who has personally recruited 350 or more Minutemen into the Brigade;

Brigadier General – A Freemason who has personally recruited 400 or more Minutemen into the Brigade;

Major General – A Freemason who has personally recruited 500 or more Minutemen into the Brigade;

Commander-in-Chief – Sorry, this rank is reserved for General Washington himself.

To progress through the different ranks, all that is required is that you personally recruit new Minutemen into the Brigade. This can be informally or formally, as there are no official "rules" for recruitment.

Recruit Service Record

1	Name	Date
	Location	Donation

2	Name	Date
	Location	Donation

3	Name	Date
	Location	Donation

4	Name	Date
	Location	Donation

5	Name	Date
	Location	Donation

6	Name	Date
	Location	Donation

7	Name	Date
	Location	Donation
8	Name	Date
	Location	Donation
9	Name	Date
	Location	Donation
10	Name	Date
	Location	Donation
11	Name	Date
	Location	Donation
12	Name	Date
	Location	Donation
13	Name	Date
	Location	Donation
14	Name	Date
	Location	Donation

15	Name		Date
	Location		Donation

16	Name		Date
	Location		Donation

17	Name		Date
	Location		Donation

18	Name		Date
	Location		Donation

19	Name		Date
	Location		Donation

20	Name		Date
	Location		Donation

21	Name		Date
	Location		Donation

22	Name		Date
	Location		Donation

23	Name		Date	
Location			Donation	
24	Name		Date	
Location			Donation	
25	Name		Date	
Location			Donation	

Congratulations!
You are now a

PRIVATE

in the
George Washington Memorial Brigade!

Private Service Record

26	Name	Date
	Location	Donation

27	Name	Date
	Location	Donation

28	Name	Date
	Location	Donation

29	Name	Date
	Location	Donation

30	Name	Date
	Location	Donation

31	Name	Date
	Location	Donation

32	Name	Date
	Location	Donation

33	Name	Date
	Location	Donation

34	Name	Date
	Loc35ation	Donation

35	Name	Date
	Location	Donation

36	Name	Date
	Location	Donation

37	Name	Date
	Location	Donation

38	Name	Date
	Location	Donation

39	Name	Date
	Location	Donation

	Name	Date
40		
Location		Donation

	Name	Date
41		
Location		Donation

	Name	Date
42		
Location		Donation

	Name	Date
43		
Location		Donation

	Name	Date
44		
Location		Donation

	Name	Date
45		
Location		Donation

	Name	Date
46		
Location		Donation

	Name	Date
47		
Location		Donation

48	Name		Date	
	Location		Donation	

49	Name		Date	
	Location		Donation	

50	Name		Date	
	Location		Donation	

Congratulations!
You are now a

CORPORAL

in the
George Washington Memorial Brigade!

Corporal Service Record

51	Name	Date
	Location	Donation

52	Name	Date
	Location	Donation

53	Name	Date
	Location	Donation

54	Name	Date
	Location	Donation

55	Name	Date
	Location	Donation

56	Name	Date
	Location	Donation

57	Name	Date
	Loc58ation	Donation
58	Name	Date
	Location	Donation
59	Name	Date
	Location	Donation
60	Name	Date
	Location	Donation
61	Name	Date
	Location	Donation
62	Name	Date
	Location	Donation
63	Name	Date
	Location	Donation
64	Name	Date
	Location	Donation

65	Name	Date
	Location	Donation

66	Name	Date
	Location	Donation

67	Name	Date
	Location	Donation

68	Name	Date
	Location	Donation

69	Name	Date
	Location	Donation

70	Name	Date
	Location	Donation

71	Name	Date
	Location	Donation

72	Name	Date
	Location	Donation

73	Name		Date	
	Location		Donation	
74	Name		Date	
	Location		Donation	
75	Name		Date	
	Location		Donation	

Congratulations!
You are now a

SERGEANT

in the
George Washington Memorial Brigade!

Sergeant Service Record

76	Name	Date
	Location	Donation

77	Name	Date
	Location	Donation

78	Name	Date
	Location	Donation

79	Name	Date
	Location	Donation

80	Name	Date
	Location	Donation

81	Name	Date
	Location	Donation

82	Name	Date
	Location	Donation

83	Name	Date
	Location	Donation

84	Name	Date
	Location	Donation

85	Name	Date
	Location	Donation

86	Name	Date
	Location	Donation

87	Name	Date
	Location	Donation

88	Name	Date
	Location	Donation

89	Name	Date
	Location	Donation

	Name	Date
90		
Location		Donation

	Name	Date
91		
Location		Donation

	Name	Date
92		
Location		Donation

	Name	Date
93		
Location		Donation

	Name	Date
94		
Location		Donation

	Name	Date
95		
Location		Donation

	Name	Date
96		
Location		Donation

	Name	Date
97		
Location		Donation

98	Name		Date	
	Location		Donation	

99	Name		Date	
	Location		Donation	

100	Name		Date	
	Location		Donation	

Congratulations!
You are now a

SERGEANT MAJOR

in the
George Washington Memorial Brigade!

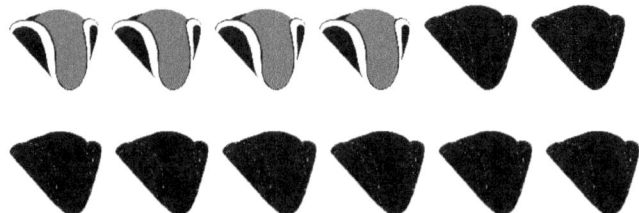

Sergeant Major Service Record

101	Name	Date
	Location	Donation

102	Name	Date
	Location	Donation

103	Name	Date
	Location	Donation

104	Name	Date
	Location	Donation

105	Name	Date
	Location	Donation

106	Name	Date
	Location	Donation

107	Name	Date
	Location	Donation

108	Name	Date
	Location	Donation

109	Name	Date
	Location	Donation

110	Name	Date
	Location	Donation

111	Name	Date
	Location	Donation

112	Name	Date
	Location	Donation

113	Name	Date
	Location	Donation

114	Name	Date
	Location	Donation

	Name	Date
115		
Location		Donation

	Name	Date
116		
Location		Donation

	Name	Date
117		
Location		Donation

	Name	Date
118		
Location		Donation

	Name	Date
119		
Location		Donation

	Name	Date
120		
Location		Donation

	Name	Date
121		
Location		Donation

	Name	Date
122		
Location		Donation

123	Name		Date
	Location		Donation
124	Name		Date
	Location		Donation
125	Name		Date
	Location		Donation

Congratulations!
You are now a

LIEUTENANT

in the
George Washington Memorial Brigade!

Lieutenant Service Record

126	Name	Date
	Location	Donation

127	Name	Date
	Location	Donation

128	Name	Date
	Location	Donation

129	Name	Date
	Location	Donation

130	Name	Date
	Location	Donation

131	Name	Date
	Location	Donation

132	Name	Date
	Location	Donation

133	Name	Date
	Location	Donation

134	Name	Date
	Location	Donation

135	Name	Date
	Location	Donation

136	Name	Date
	Location	Donation

137	Name	Date
	Location	Donation

138	Name	Date
	Location	Donation

139	Name	Date
	Location	Donation

140	Name	Date
	Location	Donation

141	Name	Date
	Location	Donation

142	Name	Date
	Location	Donation

143	Name	Date
	Location	Donation

144	Name	Date
	Location	Donation

145	Name	Date
	Location	Donation

146	Name	Date
	Location	Donation

147	Name	Date
	Location	Donation

148 Name	Date
Location	Donation

149 Name	Date
Location	Donation

150 Name	Date
Location	Donation

Congratulations!
You are now a

SUBALTERN

in the
George Washington Memorial Brigade!

Subaltern Service Record

151	Name	Date
	Location	Donation

152	Name	Date
	Location	Donation

153	Name	Date
	Location	Donation

154	Name	Date
	Location	Donation

155	Name	Date
	Location	Donation

156	Name	Date
	Location	Donation

157	Name	Date
	Location	Donation

158	Name	Date
	Location	Donation

159	Name	Date
	Location	Donation

160	Name	Date
	Location	Donation

161	Name	Date
	Location	Donation

162	Name	Date
	Location	Donation

163	Name	Date
	Location	Donation

164	Name	Date
	Location	Donation

165	Name	Date
	Location	Donation
166	Name	Date
	Location	Donation
167	Name	Date
	Location	Donation
168	Name	Date
	Location	Donation
169	Name	Date
	Location	Donation
170	Name	Date
	Location	Donation
171	Name	Date
	Location	Donation
172	Name	Date
	Location	Donation

173	Name	Date
	Location	Donation

174	Name	Date
	Location	Donation

175	Name	Date
	Location	Donation

176	Name	Date
	Location	Donation

177	Name	Date
	Location	Donation

178	Name	Date
	Location	Donation

179	Name	Date
	Location	Donation

180	Name	Date
	Location	Donation

181	Name	Date
	Location	Donation

182	Name	Date
	Location	Donation

183	Name	Date
	Location	Donation

184	Name	Date
	Location	Donation

185	Name	Date
	Location	Donation

186	Name	Date
	Location	Donation

187	Name	Date
	Location	Donation

188	Name	Date
	Location	Donation

189	Name		Date
	Location		Donation

190	Name		Date
	Location		Donation

191	Name		Date
	Location		Donation

192	Name		Date
	Location		Donation

193	Name		Date
	Location		Donation

194	Name		Date
	Location		Donation

195	Name		Date
	Location		Donation

196	Name		Date
	Location		Donation

197	Name		Date
	Location		Donation
198	Name		Date
	Location		Donation
199	Name		Date
	Location		Donation
200	Name		Date
	Location		Donation

Congratulations!
You are now a

CAPTAIN

in the
George Washington Memorial Brigade!

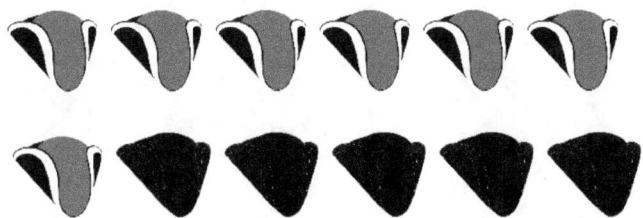

Captain Service Record

201	Name	Date
	Location	Donation

202	Name	Date
	Location	Donation

203	Name	Date
	Location	Donation

204	Name	Date
	Location	Donation

205	Name	Date
	Location	Donation

206	Name	Date
	Location	Donation

207	Name	Date
	Location	Donation

208	Name	Date
	Location	Donation

209	Name	Date
	Location	Donation

210	Name	Date
	Location	Donation

211	Name	Date
	Location	Donation

212	Name	Date
	Location	Donation

213	Name	Date
	Location	Donation

214	Name	Date
	Location	Donation

215	Name	Date
	Location	Donation

216	Name	Date
	Location	Donation

217	Name	Date
	Location	Donation

218	Name	Date
	Location	Donation

219	Name	Date
	Location	Donation

220	Name	Date
	Location	Donation

221	Name	Date
	Location	Donation

222	Name	Date
	Location	Donation

223	Name	Date
	Location	Donation

224	Name	Date
	Location	Donation

225	Name	Date
	Location	Donation

226	Name	Date
	Location	Donation

227	Name	Date
	Location	Donation

228	Name	Date
	Location	Donation

229	Name	Date
	Location	Donation

230	Name	Date
	Location	Donation

231	Name	Date
	Location	Donation

232	Name	Date
	Location	Donation

233	Name	Date
	Location	Donation

234	Name	Date
	Location	Donation

235	Name	Date
	Location	Donation

236	Name	Date
	Location	Donation

237	Name	Date
	Location	Donation

238	Name	Date
	Location	Donation

239	Name	Date
	Location	Donation

240	Name	Date
	Location	Donation

241	Name	Date
	Location	Donation

242	Name	Date
	Location	Donation

243	Name	Date
	Location	Donation

244	Name	Date
	Location	Donation

245	Name	Date
	Location	Donation

246	Name	Date
	Location	Donation

247	Name	Date
	Location	Donation

248	Name	Date
	Location	Donation

249	Name	Date
	Location	Donation

250	Name	Date
	Location	Donation

Congratulations!
You are now a

MAJOR

in the
George Washington Memorial Brigade!

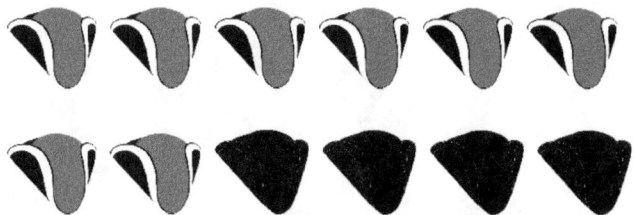

Major Service Record

	Name	Date
251		
Location		Donation

	Name	Date
252		
Location		Donation

	Name	Date
253		
Location		Donation

	Name	Date
254		
Location		Donation

	Name	Date
255		
Location		Donation

	Name	Date
256		
Location		Donation

257	Name		Date
	Location		Donation
258	Name		Date
	Location		Donation
259	Name		Date
	Location		Donation
260	Name		Date
	Location		Donation
261	Name		Date
	Location		Donation
262	Name		Date
	Location		Donation
263	Name		Date
	Location		Donation
264	Name		Date
	Location		Donation

265	Name	Date
	Location	Donation

266	Name	Date
	Location	Donation

267	Name	Date
	Location	Donation

268	Name	Date
	Location	Donation

269	Name	Date
	Location	Donation

270	Name	Date
	Location	Donation

271	Name	Date
	Location	Donation

272	Name	Date
	Location	Donation

273	Name	Date
	Location	Donation

274	Name	Date
	Location	Donation

275	Name	Date
	Location	Donation

276	Name	Date
	Location	Donation

277	Name	Date
	Location	Donation

278	Name	Date
	Location	Donation

279	Name	Date
	Location	Donation

280	Name	Date
	Location	Donation

281	Name	Date
	Location	Donation

282	Name	Date
	Location	Donation

283	Name	Date
	Location	Donation

284	Name	Date
	Location	Donation

285	Name	Date
	Location	Donation

286	Name	Date
	Location	Donation

287	Name	Date
	Location	Donation

288	Name	Date
	Location	Donation

289	Name	Date
	Location	Donation
290	Name	Date
	Location	Donation
291	Name	Date
	Location	Donation
292	Name	Date
	Location	Donation
293	Name	Date
	Location	Donation
294	Name	Date
	Location	Donation
295	Name	Date
	Location	Donation
296	Name	Date
	Location	Donation

297	Name		Date
	Location		Donation
298	Name		Date
	Location		Donation
299	Name		Date
	Location		Donation
300	Name		Date
	Location		Donation

Congratulations!
You are now a

LIEUTENANT COLONEL

in the
George Washington Memorial Brigade!

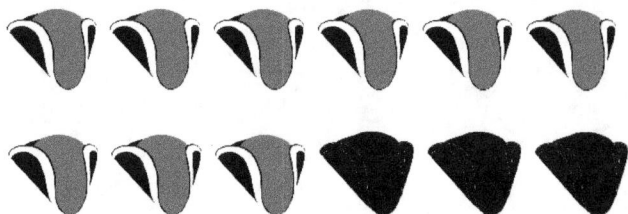

Lieutenant Colonel Service Record

301	Name	Date
	Location	Donation

302	Name	Date
	Location	Donation

303	Name	Date
	Location	Donation

304	Name	Date
	Location	Donation

305	Name	Date
	Location	Donation

306	Name	Date
	Location	Donation

307	Name	Date
	Location	Donation

308	Name	Date
	Location	Donation

309	Name	Date
	Location	Donation

310	Name	Date
	Location	Donation

311	Name	Date
	Location	Donation

312	Name	Date
	Location	Donation

313	Name	Date
	Location	Donation

314	Name	Date
	Location	Donation

315	Name	Date
	Location	Donation

316	Name	Date
	Location	Donation

317	Name	Date
	Location	Donation

318	Name	Date
	Location	Donation

319	Name	Date
	Location	Donation

320	Name	Date
	Location	Donation

321	Name	Date
	Location	Donation

322	Name	Date
	Location	Donation

323	Name	Date
	Location	Donation

324	Name	Date
	Location	Donation

325	Name	Date
	Location	Donation

326	Name	Date
	Location	Donation

327	Name	Date
	Location	Donation

328	Name	Date
	Location	Donation

329	Name	Date
	Location	Donation

330	Name	Date
	Location	Donation

331	Name	Date
	Location	Donation

332	Name	Date
	Location	Donation

333	Name	Date
	Location	Donation

334	Name	Date
	Location	Donation

335	Name	Date
	Location	Donation

336	Name	Date
	Location	Donation

337	Name	Date
	Location	Donation

338	Name	Date
	Location	Donation

339	Name		Date	
	Location		Donation	

340	Name		Date	
	Location		Donation	

341	Name		Date	
	Location		Donation	

342	Name		Date	
	Location		Donation	

343	Name		Date	
	Location		Donation	

344	Name		Date	
	Location		Donation	

345	Name		Date	
	Location		Donation	

346	Name		Date	
	Location		Donation	

347	Name		Date
	Location		Donation
348	Name		Date
	Location		Donation
349	Name		Date
	Location		Donation
350	Name		Date
	Location		Donation

Congratulations!
You are now a

COLONEL

in the
George Washington Memorial Brigade!

Colonel Service Record

351	Name	Date
	Location	Donation

352	Name	Date
	Location	Donation

353	Name	Date
	Location	Donation

354	Name	Date
	Location	Donation

355	Name	Date
	Location	Donation

356	Name	Date
	Location	Donation

357	Name	Date
	Location	Donation

358	Name	Date
	Location	Donation

359	Name	Date
	Location	Donation

360	Name	Date
	Location	Donation

361	Name	Date
	Location	Donation

362	Name	Date
	Location	Donation

363	Name	Date
	Location	Donation

364	Name	Date
	Location	Donation

365	Name	Date
	Location	Donation

366	Name	Date
	Location	Donation

367	Name	Date
	Location	Donation

368	Name	Date
	Location	Donation

369	Name	Date
	Location	Donation

370	Name	Date
	Location	Donation

371	Name	Date
	Location	Donation

372	Name	Date
	Location	Donation

373	Name	Date
	Location	Donation

374	Name	Date
	Location	Donation

375	Name	Date
	Location	Donation

376	Name	Date
	Location	Donation

377	Name	Date
	Location	Donation

378	Name	Date
	Location	Donation

379	Name	Date
	Location	Donation

380	Name	Date
	Location	Donation

381	Name	Date
	Location	Donation

382	Name	Date
	Location	Donation

383	Name	Date
	Location	Donation

384	Name	Date
	Location	Donation

385	Name	Date
	Location	Donation

386	Name	Date
	Location	Donation

387	Name	Date
	Location	Donation

388	Name	Date
	Location	Donation

389	Name	Date
	Location	Donation

390	Name	Date
	Location	Donation

391	Name	Date
	Location	Donation

392	Name	Date
	Location	Donation

393	Name	Date
	Location	Donation

394	Name	Date
	Location	Donation

395	Name	Date
	Location	Donation

396	Name	Date
	Location	Donation

397	Name		Date
	Location		Donation
398	Name		Date
	Location		Donation
399	Name		Date
	Location		Donation
400	Name		Date

Congratulations!
You are now a

BRIGADIER GENERAL

in the
George Washington Memorial Brigade!

Brigadier General Service Record

401	Name	Date
	Location	Donation

402	Name	Date
	Location	Donation

403	Name	Date
	Location	Donation

404	Name	Date
	Location	Donation

405	Name	Date
	Location	Donation

406	Name	Date
	Location	Donation

407	Name		Date
	Location		Donation

408	Name		Date
	Location		Donation

409	Name		Date
	Location		Donation

410	Name		Date
	Location		Donation

411	Name		Date
	Location		Donation

412	Name		Date
	Location		Donation

413	Name		Date
	Location		Donation

414	Name		Date
	Location		Donation

415	Name		Date
	Location		Donation

416	Name		Date
	Location		Donation

417	Name		Date
	Location		Donation

418	Name		Date
	Location		Donation

419	Name		Date
	Location		Donation

420	Name		Date
	Location		Donation

421	Name		Date
	Location		Donation

422	Name		Date
	Location		Donation

423	Name	Date
	Location	Donation

424	Name	Date
	Location	Donation

425	Name	Date
	Location	Donation

426	Name	Date
	Location	Donation

427	Name	Date
	Location	Donation

428	Name	Date
	Location	Donation

429	Name	Date
	Location	Donation

430	Name	Date
	Location	Donation

431	Name	Date
	Location	Donation

432	Name	Date
	Location	Donation

433	Name	Date
	Location	Donation

434	Name	Date
	Location	Donation

435	Name	Date
	Location	Donation

436	Name	Date
	Location	Donation

437	Name	Date
	Location	Donation

438	Name	Date
	Location	Donation

439	Name	Date
	Location	Donation

440	Name	Date
	Location	Donation

441	Name	Date
	Location	Donation

442	Name	Date
	Location	Donation

443	Name	Date
	Location	Donation

444	Name	Date
	Location	Donation

445	Name	Date
	Location	Donation

446	Name	Date
	Location	Donation

447	Name	Date
	Location	Donation

448	Name	Date
	Location	Donation

449	Name	Date
	Location	Donation

450	Name	Date
	Location	Donation

451	Name	Date
	Location	Donation

452	Name	Date
	Location	Donation

453	Name	Date
	Location	Donation

454	Name	Date
	Location	Donation

455	Name	Date
	Location	Donation

456	Name	Date
	Location	Donation

457	Name	Date
	Location	Donation

458	Name	Date
	Location	Donation

459	Name	Date
	Location	Donation

460	Name	Date
	Location	Donation

461	Name	Date
	Location	Donation

462	Name	Date
	Location	Donation

463	Name	Date
	Location	Donation

464	Name	Date
	Location	Donation

465	Name	Date
	Location	Donation

466	Name	Date
	Location	Donation

467	Name	Date
	Location	Donation

468	Name	Date
	Location	Donation

469	Name	Date
	Location	Donation

470	Name	Date
	Location	Donation

471	Name	Date
	Location	Donation
472	Name	Date
	Location	Donation
473	Name	Date
	Location	Donation
474	Name	Date
	Location	Donation
475	Name	Date
	Location	Donation
476	Name	Date
	Location	Donation
477	Name	Date
	Location	Donation
478	Name	Date
	Location	Donation

479	Name	Date
	Location	Donation

480	Name	Date
	Location	Donation

481	Name	Date
	Location	Donation

482	Name	Date
	Location	Donation

483	Name	Date
	Location	Donation

484	Name	Date
	Location	Donation

485	Name	Date
	Location	Donation

486	Name	Date
	Location	Donation

487	Name		Date
	Location		Donation

488	Name		Date
	Location		Donation

489	Name		Date
	Location		Donation

490	Name		Date
	Location		Donation

491	Name		Date
	Location		Donation

492	Name		Date
	Location		Donation

493	Name		Date
	Location		Donation

494	Name		Date
	Location		Donation

495	Name	Date
	Location	Donation
496	Name	Date
	Location	Donation
497	Name	Date
	Location	Donation
498	Name	Date
	Location	Donation
499	Name	Date
	Location	Donation
500	Name	Date

Congratulations!
You are now a

MAJOR GENERAL

in the
George Washington Memorial Brigade!

One of
General Washington's
Own!

ABOUT THE AUTHOR

The Author is a Freemason, Past Master,
and, most of all, an American Patriot.

He hopes YOU are
an American Patriot as well!

SO·MOTE·IT·BE

www.ingramcontent.com/pod-product-compliance
Lightning Source LLC
Chambersburg PA
CBHW070118290526
45789CB00005B/2061